POETIC PORTRAITS

Edited By Lynsey Evans

First published in Great Britain in 2024 by:

YoungWriters®
— Est. 1991 —

Young Writers
Remus House
Coltsfoot Drive
Peterborough
PE2 9BF
Telephone: 01733 890066
Website: www.youngwriters.co.uk

Printed and bound in the UK by BookPrintingUK
Website: www.bookprintinguk.com
YB0573O

FOREWORD

For Young Writers' latest competition This Is Me,
we asked primary school pupils to look inside
themselves, to think about what makes them unique,
and then write a poem about it! They rose to the
challenge magnificently and the result is this fantastic
collection of poems in a variety of poetic styles.

Here at Young Writers our aim is to encourage creativity
in children and to inspire a love of the written word, so
it's great to get such an amazing response, with some
absolutely fantastic poems. It's important for children to
focus on and celebrate themselves and this competition
allowed them to write freely and honestly, celebrating
what makes them great, expressing their hopes and
fears, or simply writing about their favourite things.
This Is Me gave them the power of words. The result
is a collection of inspirational and moving poems that
also showcase their creativity and writing ability.

I'd like to congratulate all the young poets
in this anthology, I hope this inspires them
to continue with their creative writing.

THE POEMS

Refuge

I go to my sister's room to eat her sweets,
Munch! Munch! Munch!
I leave no trace of her treats.
She comes marching down the stairs,
Stomp! Stomp! Stomp!
She's going to turn into a bear,
I run to my tree house, my heartbeat rising.
I lie on my couch,
Gradually dazing.
I wake up hearing shouts of my name,
My eardrums are going through so much pain,
I hear my sister stomping away.
I'm watching Mukbangs,
I think what a beautiful day,
No need to worry about my sister screaming,
I see the moon slowly beaming.
I always feel safe here,
When I'm in the sanctuary of my blanket.

Chensu Gurung (10)
Cedars Manor School, Harrow

Monster Under My Bed!

I got up from my bed,
I heard a scary sound,
That was when I saw,
What was sitting next to me?

It was a hairy monster,
Twice the size of me,
Whilst looking down on me,
I felt like a humble bee.

My instincts told me to run,
But I just ate a bun.

In the end, I ran,
Which was a perfect plan
I was running and hiding,
Goosebumps head to toe.

I went to my parent's room,
Told them what happened,
Was it my imagination?
In the end, it was like animation.

Safe in my parent's room
Now everything is okay,
Hoping for the best
The very next day!

Robert Boca (11)
Cedars Manor School, Harrow

Refuge!

Look around
You're not proud

Make a sound
Ahhh! No one's there

Look up - nothing's there - nothing's there
Nothing's there

Look ahead, look down
Nothing's there
But your feet are there

Earth is so big and so is this room
I'd hate to use a broom
The whispers of others swirl around you
But no one's there - no one's there

Maybe, maybe, maybe
That place and the whispers were not a dream

But you've arrived
You're alive

At home - in peace
Your ultimate trust.

Eduan Kashtanjeva (10)
Cedars Manor School, Harrow

Refuge!

Screaming, screaming everywhere!
With all this noise I can't bear
On my way to find peace and quiet
All this extreme running is making me tired.

Finally, I find a quiet room
Then suddenly, I hear a *boom!*

Children crying everywhere!
Shouting, hitting and pulling hair
I have to find a way out
All this noise is making me shout.

I find a bike
That I really like

I finally find a place to stay
I'm really tired, I must say
I have a cup of tea
I look outside and see...

Peace!

Asiya Yassin (10)
Cedars Manor School, Harrow

Thunder And Lightning

Pitter-patter, pitter-patter... whoosh!
It's pouring. It's pouring
It's raining cats and dogs
My wellies are oceans
I'm wet from head to toe
Run, run, run!
I'm running, I'm running
I'm running from the rain
Crash, crackle, boom!
Thunder and lightning
Lightning and thunder
Coming after me
Finally, finally I've reached my door
It's cosy inside
Hot cocoa
On my sofa
All dry now
I'm warm! I'm cosy! I'm safe!

Mia Pindoria (10)
Cedars Manor School, Harrow

This Is Me

You might have gigantic worries but you can't just stay.
If you're anxious, just put relaxing music on.
Try to balance, don't collapse from tiredness.
If you feel like your heart will jump out of your chest, think of something else.
Don't be ashamed of yourself.
If you sob every day and night, try to stop.
If your heart's beating rapidly, breathe in and breathe out.
If you're depressed, don't think you're weird.
No time to be emotional, you've just got to go.

Safaya Samrai (7)
Cedars Manor School, Harrow

In The Deep

I dive into water - I start to sink
My eyes start to burn - is this the end?
I see a light, will I be okay
Or will this be my last day?
I try to hold my breath, I need to let go.

I wake up - my heartbeat is slow
I open my eyes and can see everything around me
I can finally breathe
I think I'm okay.

Until it starts to rain, water trickles down on me
I'm no longer dry, I'm now wet
I run for cover under a tree,
I'm finally free, free, free.

Iliyas Nazar (10)
Cedars Manor School, Harrow

Beginning Of A Refugee

T he refugees travel by cars and planes, they might even walk.

H ome to home.

E scaping floods, earthquakes and conflict.

R unning towards a better life.

E ven though they don't have a home, they might still have a family.

F amily is there for them.

U nknown places await them.

G irls and boys still might have parents.

E veryone is hungry.

E lements against them.

S ome refugees walk for many days.

Molly Fischer (7)
Cedars Manor School, Harrow

Home At Last

Home at last,
Splish, splash, squelch,
Rain pours freely,
Hail bounces off the ground,
Everyone is soaked, it starts to snow,
Snowballs fly out of people's hands,
This winter war has begun,
Ice slides down your neck,
You get hit in the face,
You must get out!
The bus is leaving,
Quick, catch it!
Mum is at home, waiting with tea,
You jump on the bus, just before it leaves,
Hours pass and you're home at last,
Drinking your tea.

Bawery Pedawi (10)
Cedars Manor School, Harrow

This Is Me

It's time to leave,
Nothing will save you.
No time to cry or grieve,
Leave lots of things that will never leave your heart.
Crying into your pillow won't help your situation.
Tremble and creep all night and day,
Can't sleep, can't eat.
Huge teardrops take a while to dry on your pillow,
You are really just helpless!
Get a plane and walk it through.
In a car, speeding away from home.
Can't take ten suitcases, can't bring all your family.

Kelvi Rathod (7)
Cedars Manor School, Harrow

Social Anxiety

Outside I go
They're no people around
Finally I can calm down
As I walk down the street
I hear murmurs coming towards me

I see no one's there
Deciding to walk down
I hear voices of doubt
Shall I go?
Chatter... Chatter... Chatter...

My heart beats like a drum
I start to run as fast as a rabbit
Stomp... Crunch... Scream...

At last, I arrive home
Once again I am safe
In my place of haven.

Aliya Abdow (11)
Cedars Manor School, Harrow

Refuge

Rain pouring down on me
How wet I could be
Can't believe I could see
Rain pouring down endlessly

Rain pouring down on me
How wet I could be
Can't believe I could see
Rain pouring down endlessly

Stand under a tree
Bees surrounding me
Finally, protection from the rain
Oh no! A drop touched my head
I need to run again

Get home in my bed
Make tea and have a sip
Look outside
Drip! Drip! Drip!

Auswa Noori (10)
Cedars Manor School, Harrow

Saint George

S lowly sauntering into a land of joy.

A m I dreaming, or is this real?

I t has so many Starbucks stalls.

N ever in my life have I frowned there.

T ornados are strong, but my love for Saint George is more grand.

G o for a drink, maybe an...

E nergising one!

O h wow! Look at those rides!

R umbling stomachs all around.

G etting food from Harriet's helps.

E njoying the company!

Nuriya Sayfullaeva (8)
Cedars Manor School, Harrow

My Garden

M y swing slowly swinging to the rhythm of the air
Y ellow flowers dancing in their pots, dancing like ballerinas

G reen grass sleeping in the cold, blistering wind
A coloured big ball waiting patiently to be kicked
R unning around and carefully throwing the ball to my friend
D ried out dead flowers, almost everywhere
E nding my day with a quick run around
N ever have I ever not loved my wonderful garden.

Ayah Alrashid (10)

Cedars Manor School, Harrow

Refuge

Drip, drip, drip
It has started to rain
My nightmare's begun
Running, running, running
Have to find shelter
Can't wait for another second
Splash, splash, splash
Children running away screaming for help
Cats meowing and dogs barking
I don't understand why it has to rain today
Run, run, run
Finally I have found my haven
Dry and safe
Drinking my warm glass of milk.

Mahir Shah (10)
Cedars Manor School, Harrow

War

One step fading away
A new one rising

Crowds all around
But no peace to be found

Looking out at the distance
Looking out for planes

Looking back at the village
My home is now ruined

If we get there in time
I will tell my story

I'm now at my haven
I'm now safe from war

I hope to make peace
I hope to make peace
I will make peace.

Jessica Sziebert (10)
Cedars Manor School, Harrow

Refuge!

It is raining cats and dogs
Everyone is drenched to the chin
Looking for cover around the neighbourhood

Drip - Drip - Drip
Is all I hear
Hail starts, the storm begins

Splash - Splash - Splash
I must get home
My shoes are ruined
Mum is waiting

I made it home
Soaked from head to toe
With cocoa on the go
I'm safe.

Nanshika Srivathsan (10)
Cedars Manor School, Harrow

Loneliness

All alone in my room
Quiet as a mouse
I take a look around
No one is here, no one is there, no one is anywhere

Feeling isolated
Like a lone wolf
No one's here
No one's anywhere

People coming towards me
I hear voices of doubt
Shall I go?

As I go I make friends
Finally I'm not alone
I'm not alone
I'm not alone.

Hussain Thalmawi (11)
Cedars Manor School, Harrow

Out Of The Dark

In the deep, dark silence
I lie down, waiting for something
The horrible smell of flint
Consumes my nose.

Bang! Bang! Bang!
Stomp! Stomp! Stomp!

Hiding from the monster
Waiting for hope
Waiting for help.

Running home
Drinking a cup of tea
I'm safe, I'm safe.

Modasir Amani (10)
Cedars Manor School, Harrow

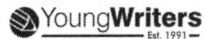

Refugees

T hey came to my house
H iding and about
E nemies around

R iding and walking
E vening on a different land
F light, taking a flight
U nder the sun
G round at last
E ventually in a school
E ntering a new house
S afe and sound.

Sarah Salim (7)
Cedars Manor School, Harrow

Oak Tree

O n the green sturdy tree
A ppears a shadow that calms me
K eeping me warm, keeping me safe

T ouching the leaves, letting me relax
R esting as always, next to the branch
E nergising my soul, to climb up the tree
E verywhere acorns falling all over me!

Melissa Georgeta Costea (8)
Cedars Manor School, Harrow

My Bed!

M y head rests on a puffy surface known as my plumped pillow

Y ou would feel like you were in heaven in the depths of my bed

B lankets as soft as clouds cover my toes

E normous sheets rest upon me

D reams dance into my head as I slowly drift away in the comfort of my bed!

Safiya Sayfullaeva (10)
Cedars Manor School, Harrow

My Bedroom

M ajestic and marvellous.
Y ellow and king-sized.

B eautiful and comfy.
E arned to relax.
D inosaur pillows.
R ealistic armadillos.
O h, the peace and quiet.
O h, how I love to skip into a world of
M agical dreams.

Srimuhil Prasanna (8)
Cedars Manor School, Harrow

Refuge!

I woke up from my bed
My house was now debris
I looked outside my window
Shells falling from the sky
The bomb slammed on the floor
I saw fire on the ground
I took slow steps to my van
Boom! Blast! Pow!
I accelerated to another city
Finally, a place of haven.

Ali Ahmed Moazzam (10)
Cedars Manor School, Harrow

My Mum And Me

My mum and I cuddle together,
In the warm and cosy weather.
It makes me feel safe,
My mum is cool.
Whilst my mum and I listen to calm music,
We watch the beautiful sunset.
We both tell jokes to each other,
I always make her laugh.
This is my special place.

Tiyah John-Lewis (8)
Cedars Manor School, Harrow

Refuge!

Bang!
Running away again,
Leaving all memories behind,
No looking back,
Take the bus,
Take the train,
Take everything possible to escape,
Don't stop until you feel safe,
Finally, I've found a place,
My forever home,
Forever.

Eliza-Elena Iorgu (10)
Cedars Manor School, Harrow

Arcade

A rcades are explosive fun!

R ides and games, making your head dizzy!

C otton candy cravings creep up on me!

A claw machine, ready to pounce! Better win that toy.

D ancing energetically to tunes.

E ager to win mini-golf!

Simran Laxman (8)

Cedars Manor School, Harrow

India

If you want my refuge,
India is the place.
Not because it's my home,
But because of its good features.

Dance class,
Good homework,
A society filled with happiness.

Simple sequences
Tough chess
Monopoly is the richest.

Ved Pathak (8)
Cedars Manor School, Harrow

Art Room

A rt room is my refuge
R apidly sharpening pencils
T rying to make the best painting

R olling clay, moulding away!
O pening a rainbow palette
O h my gosh, pencils snap at me!
M asterpiece before me!

Myra Ahuja (8)
Cedars Manor School, Harrow

Harrow

H igh-speed trains in the underground
A couple of difficult tunnels
R aging ferries
R ed, ripe apples in the trees
O verhead might be a plane or two
W andering people in the towns.

Alexander Druteiko (8)

Cedars Manor School, Harrow

My Room

Cuddling under
My candyfloss pillow
Snuggling with teddy
Who snores

Bright sunshine
Floods the room
Playing with my silly billy toys
Wrapped in a
Tortilla blanket.

Elisa-Maria Loluta (8)
Cedars Manor School, Harrow

My Bedroom

My bedroom!
My sunny, bubbly place
My refuge!
Cotton candy blanket
Protecting from worries
Pillows like clouds
Drifting dreams
Hiding from parents
Nobody can see me.

Dhyana Padhya (8)
Cedars Manor School, Harrow

Grandma's House

Grandma's house is my refuge
Delicious smells of rice and soup fill every room
Non, the cat snuggling on the couch
Sultan racing cars in the living room
Laughter makes me feel safe.

Sami Gaber (9)
Cedars Manor School, Harrow

Refuge!

R unning away from my brother
E arly in the morning
F riends waiting outside
U nder the tree
G iggling
E xcited, we went to the fair.

Matei Dumitru (10)

Cedars Manor School, Harrow

Blanket

Wraps me up,
Warm and fluffy.
Hides from parents,
Soothing and comfy.
Playing on my tablet,
Escaping the world.
In my blanket,
I am all curled up.

Kairav Mattoo (8)
Cedars Manor School, Harrow

This Is Me!

To make me you will need:
6 rocks (I talk to rocks)
A piece of bark
A sprinkle of happy and crazy
A sprouting oak tree
Crumbled ivy leaves
A climbing harness (to get the leaves)
3 sweets and a cup of mango
A mug of caffeine-free latte
1 teddy (to cuddle)
A cup of tea with four sugars
Wolf hair
Capidara hair
A load of art supplies
Cheesy pizza
A 4ml cup of coconut
A 6ml cup of melted chocolate
Kitten fur
Dog fur
A shed for my leopard yellow gecko

Guinea pig fur
1 chicken nugget

Mix them together randomly (because I am random)
But make sure you are smiling and joyful.

Amber Polley (9)

Cheriton Bishop Community Primary School, Cheriton Bishop

To Create Me

To create me you need:
5 mangoes
3 sweets
Green tea with five sugars
Cheese pizza
Choc chip cookies
School
Gymnastics
Water
Lip balm
1 teddy
Some ice
1 bird feather
Earrings

Put some mangoes in a pot.
Put some cheese pizza in with the green tea, plus
one cup of water.
Then sprinkle all the school and gymnastics,
Put one or two huggles depending how talky you
want me.
Add the lip balm and the cookies.

Pour the teddy in,
Add earrings plus ice with the bird feather.
Mix me together,
Put me in the fridge.
Wait 30 minutes and I will be ready.

Eden Stone (9)
Cheriton Bishop Community Primary School, Cheriton Bishop

How To Bake Me

To bake me you need:
A messy bedroom
2 plates of chips
5 buckets of salt
A sprinkle of spice
A bolt of lightning
A medium-sized ice cube
A bucket of seawater
And human souls.

Now you need to:
Place your bucket of seawater
Stir the saltwater whilst adding the salt buckets
Then wait for the salt to dissolve
Pour in the spice and softly mix
Whilst mixing, drop in the bedroom
Then throw the souls before they escape
Put in the lightning bolt to stir them and mix
Then put in the chips and medium-sized ice cube
and add the spice
And finally, this is me!

Sebby Baxendale-Nichols (9)
Cheriton Bishop Community Primary School, Cheriton Bishop

Random Stuff

In the morning I am lively
Sometimes I am lazy.

At school I am funny.
On Wednesday I do my work but on Thursdays
I catch a bug and so this is me.

Red and indigo not blue but orange with a cherry
on top.
I like planting and swimming galore,
Everything blue comes knocking at my door.

Isabelle Down (9)
Cheriton Bishop Community Primary School, Cheriton Bishop

How To Make Me Happy

Eat a sandwich in forty seconds
Dunk your head in icy water
Get horse hair, or cat hair, or dog hair
Drink coffee when it's cold!
Eat two big spoonfuls of black pepper
Scare Mrs Ley, my teacher.

Do that in one day.
Mixing together these ingredients will make me
happy.

Etta Williams (10)
Cheriton Bishop Community Primary School, Cheriton Bishop

This Is Me!

T ech decks are fun
H onda Civic is my favourite car
I nterested in joining the army
S crambling on my dirt bike

I love pizza!
S hoes must be DC

M y best drink is Prime
E nergy is what it gives me.

Harry Collins (9)
Cheriton Bishop Community Primary School, Cheriton Bishop

Me

T he animals are cute.
H ave three dogs.
I love crabbing.
S o much fun reading is.

I like home-made sushi.
S o many amazing games.

M y brother is super fun.
E xciting nature.

Erin Palfrey (9)

Cheriton Bishop Community Primary School, Cheriton Bishop

This Is Me

T rying my best is my goal
H ide from my sister
I ncredible gymnast
S uper reading

I nteresting thinker
S mile no matter what

M agic maker
E ver forever this is me.

Gracie Martin (9)
Cheriton Bishop Community Primary School, Cheriton Bishop

This Is Me

T ry scorer
H ip hop fan
I nter hater
S porty

I 'm good at footy
S now hater

M ulti-sport lover
E ating machine.

Eddie Carr (9)
Cheriton Bishop Community Primary School, Cheriton Bishop

This Is Me

T alkative to friends
H ungry for food
I nterested in cars
S porty

I really like gaming
S weets are tasty

M ust have Orangina
E at mac 'n' cheese.

George Harrop (10)
Cheriton Bishop Community Primary School, Cheriton Bishop

This Is Me

T he weirdo
H appy
I nterested in nature
S plits in the playground

I like animals
S id is my dog

M y family is *amazing*
E nergetic.

Ava Charlton (9)
Cheriton Bishop Community Primary School, Cheriton Bishop

My Advice

T ake a

H at

I f it's hot

S o that you don't hurt your eyes

I f

S omething happens to your eyes, don't blame

M e

E ver.

Emelia Taylor (10)
Cheriton Bishop Community Primary School, Cheriton Bishop

This Is Me

Football player
Good sprinter
Quad biker
Bike peddler
Football lover

Tomatoes are nice
Happy and exciting
I am a good runner
Supra MK4 car
Multi-sports
Eat steaks.

Jacob Harling (10)

Cheriton Bishop Community Primary School, Cheriton Bishop

This Is Me

T hankful
H elpful
I ndependent
S mart

I ntrepid
S avage

M eticulous
E ducated.

Evie Halsey (10)
Cheriton Bishop Community Primary School, Cheriton Bishop

This Is Me

Go-kart phenomenon
Cheesy chips craver
Fitness lover
Hobox dirty fries eater
Good footballer
Mango enjoyer.

Bow Pearce (10)
Cheriton Bishop Community Primary School, Cheriton Bishop

This Is Me

I am very, very chatty
I like singing, dancing and acting
I am honest
I am kind
I love Christmas
I am very apologetic because I just feel sorry for everything
I love being me because you should never try to be anybody else
You are you and that is the best thing to do
Just be you
I am passionate about walking my dog
Because I like to get out into the countryside
And enjoy some fresh air in my lungs.

William Cox (9)
Forest Way School, Coalville

This Is Me

I am helpful
I like doing riddles and puzzles because it gives me
a challenge
I am good at swimming
I like sleeping because it's relaxing
My favourite sport is football because it's fun to
learn skills
My much-loved game is Roblox because I like
building in the game
I'm a fast runner
This is me.

Jack Marshall (10)
Forest Way School, Coalville

This Is Me

I am decent at Fortnite.
I am connected to technology.
I love all the food in the world.
My friends are awesome because they play with me.
Teachers are great because they make me smarter.
'Where's Wally?' is the best, because I can find Wally.
This is me.

Bobby Joseph (10)
Forest Way School, Coalville

This Is Me

J umping in my pool
O swald is my favourite character
S titch is a Disney movie
H istory, the topic of World War Two was good
U sing stop motion to make films
A rmy men soldiers are my toys.

Joshua Green (8)
Forest Way School, Coalville

This Is Me

I am a pro at building Lego stop motion
I am a great player at tag because I am fast
I am super at playing Minecraft because it is fun
I enjoy puzzles because puzzles are exciting
This is me!

Dylan O'Rourke (8)
Forest Way School, Coalville

This Is Me

I am great at playing with my dog
I like Christmas because it is cool
I like swimming because it is refreshing
I am awesome at fixing things.

Oscar Cave (11)
Forest Way School, Coalville

Marley

M arvellous

A mazing

R ough and tumble play

L oved

E nthusiastic

Y oga girl!

Marley Bott-Hillier (6)

Forest Way School, Coalville

Baby Cat

B lack

A rty

B ig

Y ellow

C aring

A wesome

T alented.

Jacob Allen (7)

Forest Way School, Coalville

This Is Me

I love Minecraft
I love Radio 1
I love playing at home
I am good
I love listening to music.

Jenson Hale (8)
Forest Way School, Coalville

Rose!

R eally good!
O ctober is the best!
S ome chocolate!
E nd of the story!

Rose Maddin (7)

Forest Way School, Coalville

Aadya

A mazing

A rty

D elightful

Y oung

A wesome.

Aadya Naik (8)

Forest Way School, Coalville

Jack

J olly
A mazing
C lever
K id.

Jack Elliott (5)

Forest Way School, Coalville

All About Me!

Smart, hard-working
At maths I excel
I do geography well
And have a historical spell.

I love my cool cat
And my dramatic dog.

I sprint, I run
And love doing athletics
I'm enthusiastic about football
And go to games all the time.

Family, friends
They mean so much to me
Spending time with them is a guarantee.

School is the best
As with learning I am obsessed.

So this is me
From what I see
But you don't have to agree.

Tyler Philip (11)
Lairhillock Primary School, Netherley

This Is Me

My life is like the weather, sometimes bad, sometimes good
I'm shy but always friendly and sporty but I can be lazy

I do my highland dancing and I enter competitions
I sometimes do really well and sometimes I don't but I never give up

I'm kind and very hard-working and I always try my best
Although when it comes to speaking I'm not the best

I love my cats, they're always there for me
My family is always supportive and my friends are very caring
Even though they're crazy I love them all so

I've a lovely life, I almost always have a smile
I'm full of laughter and love,
My family's been through a lot but we never give up

When I grow up I hope to be a vet
I hope to help animals and do all my very best
Animals are very caring and ever so cute
They're my life

I love to share my story but sadly I have to go
I will hopefully see you again
I hope this is not the end.

Emily Bird (11)
Lairhillock Primary School, Netherley

This Is Me

T his is me and I want you to see all about my personality

H appiness and kindness are my two goals. I will be them wherever I go

I love my family so very much. Laughing and helping even when it gets tough

S ongs are my peace, they help me calm down. When it plays I can never frown

I put thought into everything I do

S chool helps me learn and school is cool

M ost importantly I want you to know

E verything that I have I am grateful for.

Ryan Donald (11)

Lairhillock Primary School, Netherley

This Is Me

Baking is my favourite
I love my cakes and bakes.
Sports I enjoy
I want to be an athlete.
I love the sun
And the hot dogs it brings.
Snow makes me grumble
But I endure it with a wink.
I love my animals
All the fur and feathers, the *squawks*, *meows* and *barks*.

My mum's side lives in England
My dad's live here with us.
I want to see the world
I don't care when or how.
Sadly this is the end
Of the poem about me.

Ziggy Carinal (11)
Lairhillock Primary School, Netherley

This Is Me

Sophie likes K-pop but not J-pop
She is funny but not scummy
She likes horror but not The Smurfs
She likes art but she isn't smart
She likes lines because she's fine (crazy)

S hameless
O rganism
P erson
H appy
I mpassive
E xpensive

L oved
A rtistic
I ncredible
N eighbour
G raceful.

Sophie Laing (11)

Lairhillock Primary School, Netherley

This Is Me

I 'm imaginative and creative
S o, so nice and hard-working
A mazing at kickboxing
V ery determined at times
E lectricals are really cool
L emonade is my favourite drink
A ctive and I love a good adventure

L oyal
A rtistic
I ncredible
R esponsible
D etermined.

Isavela Laird (10)

Lairhillock Primary School, Netherley

This Is Me

Exchanging love with a single glance,
Reflective eyes with shapes that dance.
I do not envy, I do not boast
Docile, sweet and passionate to those I love most.
Shy and reserved when meeting a guest.
Raring to go or ready to rest.
A beam of light in the eyes of all.

Beatriz Ferreira Grecco (11)
Lairhillock Primary School, Netherley

Untitled

A rtistic
M ischievous
E xcited
L oved
I mpressive

C aring
A thletic
R espectful
L ikable
I ncredible
L oyal
E pic.

Ameli Carlile (11)

Lairhillock Primary School, Netherley

Frogs And Pasta

I like frogs
Their skin is like a swamp
I like the way they jump
Frogs are cool, I like them all
If I had a frog, I would have a ball
Other than frogs, my favourite thing is pasta
With pesto.

Teddy Sutherland (11)
Lairhillock Primary School, Netherley

How To Be Me!

Wake up in the morning, tired yawn
Maybe it's a school day
Let's make that a "No"
Watching TV, "Boring"
Giving a hug to my dog
He licks my cheek, "Aw!"
Eating breakfast, still in my pyjamas
Hang on, I'm not even eating anything!
Toast some waffles
Actually no, make that scrambled eggs
Don't want to drink my milk, "Ugh"
Time to change!
Joggers or shorts?
Jumper or crop?
Let's make it a jumper and some shorts
This poem is way too long
I'll end it here, hang on!
Let me change the name to
"How To Be Me (In The Morning)"
I'm happy now!

Ariana McCartney (10)
Parkfield Primary School, Taunton

This Is Me

January jumping
February friends
March mayhem
April Ada
Manic May
June, just my birthday
Juggling July
Amber August
October obsessive
November nature
December Darcey

Red Rowan
Fluorescent Fred
Amber Anna, Ariana and Amelia
Crazy Koa
Blue Bailey
Happy Holly
Indigo Inaya
Emerald Elliot
Purple Priya.

I am jumping
I have friends
I cause mayhem
I have a GSD Ada
I have manic Mondays
I have a birthday in June
I love juggling clowns
I love amber, orange and green
I am obsessive
I love nature
I have a sister called Darcey.

I am friends with Rowan, Fred, Anna, Koa, Bailey, Amelia, Elliot, Holly, Ariana, Inaya, Elliot and Priya. This is me.

Lois Cordier (10)
Parkfield Primary School, Taunton

This Is Me

I'm as happy as I ever could be,
As I love playing football next to the sea,
I love playing rugby,
Try, try, try,
Cricket is fun,
With wickets being taken,
Swimming is fun,
Whilst swimming freestyle.

I love watching movies,
Whilst drinking warm hot chocolates,
I love a slice of pizza in the bowling alley,
I would love a treat dinner on a special day.

I am not so happy,
When I lose a football match,
Get hit hard to the ground,
And bowl a no-ball.

I love my idol,
A mega sports star,
He's a goal machine,

And he's won the Champions League,
He's called Erling Haaland,
And he's Man City's main man up front.

Max Mannari (10)
Parkfield Primary School, Taunton

This Is Me!

A relaxing sensation under the hot sun
A hot sip of hot chocolate while huddled up in my
blankets on a cold winter's day
Happy cards and sweet greetings from all around
This must be *me!*

Afternoon tea with delicious biscuits and lots of
merriment
Christmas carols and Mum pretending she made
the Christmas turkey
Out of the blue, a loud voice shouted, "Wake up,
you gotta go to school"
The cards, laughter, biscuits and hot chocolate all
disappeared.

All the miserable school days, cold wind, yellow
leaves and homework came back
It was all just a dream
This must not be *me!*

Hannah Binoy (10)
Parkfield Primary School, Taunton

Me, Myself, And I

Inaya
Strong, smart, confident, competitive,
I'm sassy, I'm adventurous,
I'm kind but don't get on my nerves,
I do ballet but also boxing,
Try and kidnap me, you'll get what you deserve,
If that's not enough, what about jiu-jitsu?
Is that enough for you?

But not to worry, I love sleeping and puppies too
I love parties and skincare and games of risky truth
or dare?
I sit on the couch with my blanket and heater,
Feeling warm and cosy and getting sleepier.
I get ready for bed and disappear under the
sheets,
But at midnight I go downstairs
For a late-night treat.

Inaya Parakala (10)
Parkfield Primary School, Taunton

This Is Who I Am

I like to keep tidy
I don't mind a little comedy
I love art
I like to keep my heart pumping with excitement
You can make me with a spoonful of kindness
Or, 70 grams of joyfulness
There is someone in my life, she made me feel courage
No matter if you're scared to go in the ocean
Just do what you do
Just don't let that stop you
Happy, excited, courageous, sensitive, joy
Kind, smart, smiling, blue, supportive
This is me
This is who I am
I smell like mango, I eat it a lot
I have long blonde hair
My eyes are dark blue
This is me!

Holly Smart (10)
Parkfield Primary School, Taunton

All About Priya

Happy, smiley, sad, crying
Moody, grumpy, silly, jealous
Daring, kind, excited, scared
Funny, lively, worried, melancholy

Personality - sugar, funny, smiling
Sharing, caring, eggs, daring
Sweet - honey, spicy, chilly
Plain ice cream, strawberry delight

Blue, brown, green, indigo
Purple, black, gold, white
Red, pink, pale, blonde
Brunette, grey, orange, yellow

Autumn leaves falling from trees
Winter breeze, snow falling with ease
Trees green and tall
Now summer's come around again.

Priya White (10)
Parkfield Primary School, Taunton

My Bedroom

It makes me feel calm
It's beautiful, pretty, peaceful and quiet so much.
I snuggle up tight more than ever when I giggle.
It's a nice place to be when you're home alone not too far, just perfect
I love my bedroom as a lovely zone to be
When nobody can hear and see
It's a perfect place to be
I have a gruesome snooze in it sleepily
I like I get to calm myself down like koalas.
It's late so it's time to say goodbye to the day
It's so snuggly, wrapped up tight for the next day.

Philip Eamer (8)
Parkfield Primary School, Taunton

The Joy

H appy
O pen-hearted
L ittle
L ovely and likeable
Y outhful.

I'm happy and hopeful and I won't give up
I am open-hearted to the ones who love me
But I'm also open-hearted to all
I'm little but I won't give up easily
I'm lovely and likeable to all
I'm young and youthful but I won't give up easily
I'm Welsh and nothing stops me
From doing the things that I love
I'm an 8th-quarter Welsh.

Holly Page (7)
Parkfield Primary School, Taunton

I Owe It To My Pet

To my cuddly cat
I owe it to Shaddy
I owe you cuddles in the morning
I owe it to my pet
The alarm clock is an animal
The breakfast fuss over cat food
The meowing and purring in the morning
I owe it to my pet
The shady Shaddy at dark
The sprinting at dark
That crazy cat of mine
I owe it to my pet
Cuddles
Kisses
Sweet
Shaddy
Dribble
I owe it to my pet
Shadow
She is part of my heart,
Shaddy Shadow.

Rupert Francis (10)
Parkfield Primary School, Taunton

How To Make Me!

Add a dash of reading
I find it very fun
Pick up the colour purple
And put it in a bun
I love the food lasagne, so add a bit of that
Put in my favourite animals like a fox, spider or bat
I love the franchise Star Wars
As well as Halloween
I enjoy Harry Potter, but for Batman, I'm not too keen
Add a bit of Minecraft, because then you'll be glad
That this thing you've created doesn't look too bad.

Zachary Jones (10)
Parkfield Primary School, Taunton

How To Make Me!

If you want to know how to make me,
This is what you need to know.

This is me,
In order to make me you will need,
Ounces of football players implanted in your brain
like files on a computer.

A kilogram of music and rhythm dancing like an
aroma,
If you don't add drums then you might just end up
in a coma.

You'll need deep brown eyes, curious as a bee,
And the biggest heart you ever did see.

Ruben McEvans (10)
Parkfield Primary School, Taunton

Under The Bed

The safest place on Earth,
Where monsters can't get you,
Under the bed,
The cosy, warm bed,
Cosy and quiet,
The safest place on Earth.
Under the bed,
Your private room,
Secure and settled,
Safe and protected,
Relaxed and chilled,
I am safe,
I need no more,
It's dark and quiet,
This is the safest place on Earth,
Under the bed.

Jyotsna Anbuchezian (7)
Parkfield Primary School, Taunton

Don't Worry, Be Happy

When I'm glummy,
I think of my mummy.
When I'm changing Esme's nappy,
I'm not very happy.
Sometimes during the night,
I can get a big fright,
I would much prefer a movie night.
Even in the dark,
I would still enjoy the park.
My friends and family are the best,
At cheering me up if I'm sad or stressed.

Emily Pugsley (7)
Parkfield Primary School, Taunton

My School

Parkfield School is where I feel safe,
And I tell my secrets to the place.
I never feel lonely, upset or sad,
I've always got a friend to help me out.
I try to get rid of arguments about friends,
And the fun we have, it never ends.
At Parkfield, we learn and share,
And work hard through the years.

Sophie Thomas (7)
Parkfield Primary School, Taunton

In My Bedroom, I Feel Safe

My bedroom is a private place to be,
Especially when it's raining,
You can hear the rain falling on the skylights,
It sounds really relaxing,
I really like it because I get to watch it,
Dripping down the skylights,
It's really, really, really peaceful,
My bedroom is my safe zone.

Alice Pullen (7)
Parkfield Primary School, Taunton

My Favourite Person

My favourite person
Has long, beautiful blonde hair
Deep hazel eyes you can get lost in

My favourite person
Is as smart as can be just like a busy bee
Her spellings are stunning

My favourite person
Is the most beautiful person
Sincerely from your older sibling.

Elliot Lester (10)
Parkfield Primary School, Taunton

My Bedroom

My bed is comfy and warm
I can look out of the window
I see birds flying
My cat's outside
My bedroom is my private place
I can read a book on my bed
I can have a nap or play with my cat
I can listen to the birds singing
It's my safe zone
No one can hurt me.

Jacob Giles (7)
Parkfield Primary School, Taunton

My Baby Brother

I love my baby brother,
He is like no other.
We always like to play,
Every night and day.
Sometimes when he is naughty,
I go and tell Mommy.
My brother likes to eat veggie straws,
And I love curry sauce.
I will always love my baby brother,
Now and forever.

Bryce Escano (7)
Parkfield Primary School, Taunton

For Me, You Will Need:

A kind heart as red as a cherry,
Ninety-nine fine brown hairs,
Sitting on top of a chatty brain.
Just below that sits my piercing blue eyes,
That my mum says are lovely.
A spoonful of selfish jealousy
And to finish it off, a vast red nose.

Daniel Smith (10)
Parkfield Primary School, Taunton

Who I Am

I am kind,
I am happy,
I am noisy,
I am fun,
I am brave,
I am good at maths,
I am lovely,
I am pretty,
I am honest,
I respect the rules,
I go to Parkfield School,
This is me,
This is who I am,
Me, Ella.

Ella Wright (7)
Parkfield Primary School, Taunton

Me Relaxing

After school, I got to my room
To watch TV and eat my tea
After, I do my spelling in the kitchen
Then I brush my teeth
And go back to my room
Then I go to sleep
But first, I read a story
And then I go to sleep faster.

Owen Williams (7)
Parkfield Primary School, Taunton

A Dark Winter's Night

W histling

I nvisible

N ature

T rees

E erie

R aven

S nowfall

N ightmare

I cy

G oodnight

H ide

T winkling.

Frankie Mangnall (7)

Parkfield Primary School, Taunton

Isaac's House

There, I feel happy and peaceful
My best friend keeps me company too!
I feel safe with Isaac because he keeps me safe
I can rely on him too
They keep me safe and that makes me joyful
My friend is my safe place.

Jack Pope (7)
Parkfield Primary School, Taunton

Mummy's Lap

My safe place is my mummy's lap
I feel like I'm hugging a cosy teddy bear
She keeps me warm and safe
She keeps me secure and comfy
I love her so much
I feel like I am wearing a tight and cosy hug.

Bhadra Harikumar (7)
Parkfield Primary School, Taunton

On My Mummy's Lap

On my mummy's lap
It's safe and cuddly on my mummy
It's like a machine that gets rid of my emotions.
I love my mummy, she's so nice, sweet and kind.
She's like my river of peaceful love.

Rupert Salter (8)
Parkfield Primary School, Taunton

This Is Me

I will be me
My sound is loud
My hair is black
I like to draw
And I like dogs
Also, I like to cycle
A heart red as an apple
Excited as a dog
Lover of Japan
I am me.

Brayden Mendoza (10)
Parkfield Primary School, Taunton

Chilling With My Cat

I love my cats
My cats are my safe place
I have two cats
They help me with my emotions
If I feel stressed or fine
I might just want to be alone
I love chilling with my cats.

Maisie Shier (7)
Parkfield Primary School, Taunton

All About Bailey!

My dream is to inspire children,
To be them, to be free.
My role model inspired me,
She inspired many to be themselves,
To be who they want to be.
And that's my dream!

Bailey Rata (10)
Parkfield Primary School, Taunton

This Is Me!

A bit of spice and all things nice,
Bones so strong to add crunch.
Silky skin as smooth as velvet,
Active body that's always on the go.
A caring heart as sweet as can be.

Brooke Taylor (7)
Parkfield Primary School, Taunton

I Am Charlie

Charlie
Loves playing football
A tiger on the wide flanks
And a passing vision of KDB
I am a fierce fighter
Born in England
Lives in England
Charlie.

Charlie Allan (11)
Parkfield Primary School, Taunton

My Bed

My safe place is my bed
With my curtains shut
Snuggled with my teddy
It's fluffy and puffy
I lie and relax peacefully
I feel settled and we snuggle.

Betsie Williams (7)
Parkfield Primary School, Taunton

A Poem Of Me

Star Wars, books, fun
Son of Kate Moore and Steve Moore
Fan of Indiana Jones, dodgeball and Minecraft
Who feels determined
Who loves fun
Who is calm.

William Moore (10)
Parkfield Primary School, Taunton

This Is Me!

I am a star!
A star that outshines others.
Wherever I go,
There is always light.
I am a star,
A star with great determination.

Diamond Udonwaetuk (7)
Parkfield Primary School, Taunton

Wizarding World

With his glasses and his scar and his fancy new
broom
He's settling into his fancy new room.
From studying oceans to studying potions,
From digging ditches to meeting witches,
From playing in ponds to playing with wands,
It is very different in this wizarding world.

With his books and his cloak and his snowy white
owl,
He thinks that the Slytherins are extremely foul.
From doing show and tell to casting a spell,
From TV presenters to spooky Dementors,
From playing in the mud to being a half-blood,
Will he fit into this wizarding world?

Harry Davies (9)
Pentrepoeth Primary School, Bassaleg

A Smile To Start The Day

I start my day with a smile,
It becomes contagious after a while.

When I do feel a little blue,
I think of my family to get me through.

From home-made cookies,
To my dog who I wish would have lots of puppies.

So much joy that can be found,
In the simpler things, even one single pound.

There's nothing that can't be fixed,
With a belly laugh on a trip,
To the zoo to maybe see a giraffe.

I'll always be kind and fair,
I'll be sure to let you know that I care.

There's so much to see in this big world,
So turn your frown upside down.

I will aim as high as the sky,
And let nothing pass me by.

God will guide me so I'm always safe and sound,
In God we trust as it is a must!

Nicole Fensom (9)

Pentrepoeth Primary School, Bassaleg

My Poem

There once was a girl who had some spots,
A chickenpox scar, a blood blister, a wart, a lot.
She had brown hair, she had brown eyes,
But she had nothing to despise.
She had a dog called Gordon
And he was never full of boredom,
She had some chickens that were lovely and sweet,
And as a result, she didn't eat meat.
She had a mother called Kate,
She hated to be late,
She had a father called Tim,
He always wanted to win.
She lived in a little cottage, number five
And ever since then, she never felt more alive.

Isla Turley (9)
Pentrepoeth Primary School, Bassaleg

Me!

I spread my kindness to those who share,
You can listen if you dare.
I'm bendy and friendly, as fun as the sun.
So my heart stays kind around everyone.
I love to write and tell stories all day.
The joy it gives me when I write it my way.
I'm great at drawing, letting my pencil flow.
What a masterpiece you can make when you love
yourself though.
So this is me and my name is Freya.
Be kind to yourself day and night,
So remember not to fight or flight.

Freya Edelman (9)
Pentrepoeth Primary School, Bassaleg

Happiness

Happiness is a rainbow in the sky,
Happiness is a dove flying by,
Happiness is a single flower sprouting through,
Some things you never knew.

Happiness is a midsummer eve,
Happiness is climbing a tree,
Happiness is being free,
To do what you please.

Happiness at the end of your day,
You'll find happiness,
Your way.

Isabelle Howell (9)
Pentrepoeth Primary School, Bassaleg

Cheetah

C almly, she runs towards the stunned antelope.

H urriedly, it retreats towards the herd.

E xasperated, the cheetah disappears into the wilderness.

E xcitedly, she climbs a tree and pounces on a poor pigeon.

T he cheetah jumps down and falls

A sleep.

H ungry still, she wakes up looking for her next meal.

Ashleigh Kenvyn (9)

Pentrepoeth Primary School, Bassaleg

Brilliant Books

From Roald Dahl to David Walliams,
Books are brilliant,
But as one wise writer once said,
"So please, oh please, we beg, we pray,
Go throw your TV set away."
And as I would like to say,
Oh please read some decent books but some are
dirty and some are clean
But they really do gleam!

Eddie Millman (9)
Pentrepoeth Primary School, Bassaleg

Happy!

H appy is the feeling I get when

A ll my family are together. Being

P erfectly happy helps you with

P ositivity, mental health and wellbeing. It makes you say

Y es! Yay! And woohoo! Happiness is the thing we need!

Evan Rogers (9)

Pentrepoeth Primary School, Bassaleg

This Is Me

G ymnastics is so good and also good for you!

Y ou will never find a better sport, it's my fort

M y opinion: I'm the best, you can't do better, test!

N o problem, no breeze, but it's a tight squeeze

A t the gym, you learn more and more, it's impossible to stop

S o hard, but so fun, you can't stop when you're done

T he rule of the world!

I try and try and I want to win gold!

C artwheels and fun all year round

S ince the beginning, I tried and it paid off.

Charlie Crotty (9)
Petersfield CE (A) Primary School, Orwell

Christmas

C hristmas is the best time to celebrate
H erbie is the best dog ever
R iding my bike is the best
I t's the best time of the year
S o many sweets to eat
T oo many presents to open
M any friends to see
A unties and uncles are always there
S o many families and friends.

Gracie Hall (9)
Petersfield CE (A) Primary School, Orwell

All About Me

C onnie loves Christmas
H appiest time of the year
R eindeer chains clatter
I t's the best time of year
S o many sweet treats to enjoy
T he Christmas tree sparkles and shines
M assive gifts to enjoy
A lways around family
S hare gifts with my brother and sister.

Connie Ellis (9)
Petersfield CE (A) Primary School, Orwell

Christmas Spirit

C hristmas is the best time of year
H iding under my covers
R iding in his sleigh ready for the day
I ce forms over the grass
S anta comes to town
T rue stories will be told
M erry emotions cover the land
A pparently he gives presents
S now pours down on the house!

Niklas Stockley (9)
Petersfield CE (A) Primary School, Orwell

Christmas

C hristmas is the best
H appiest on Christmas Day
R unning around the tree
I ce-cold, just how I like it
S anta
T urkey
M cDonald's is the best at Christmas
A lways with family
S anta delivers presents on Christmas Day.

Dexter Ogilvie
Petersfield CE (A) Primary School, Orwell

Birthday Time

B right and sunny summer
I t's the best time of the year
R unning from the sun
T rying to get in the shade
H aving to put sun cream on
D iving into the pool
A mazing time in the sun
Y es, it's summer!

Evie Mayling (9)
Petersfield CE (A) Primary School, Orwell

I Am Musical

M usic is entertaining,
U ncommon not to like,
S ometimes it is muscle-straining,
I t brings lots of light.
C ello is a string instrument for today,
A lways wants you to train,
L ots of fun, you will say.

Clara Cunniffe (9)

Petersfield CE (A) Primary School, Orwell

It's Christmas

C hristmas is the best
H oney is the best dog
R ipping the wrapping off the presents
I like Christmas pudding
S urprise
T oys
M argo is cross
A smile
S anta.

Dolly Crotty (10)
Petersfield CE (A) Primary School, Orwell

What Sport Am I?

I'm dripping before my match,
Ready to win,
Starting to get a tiny bit nervous.
The whistle blows.
It rapidly finishes - I've won.
The nerves have left my body.

Jack Randall (9)
Petersfield CE (A) Primary School, Orwell

All About Me

Dylan is my name
Blue is my colour
Halloween is the best
Art is my game
And pizza is my fave
Running is my favourite sport
This is me.

Dylan Pennell (9)
Petersfield CE (A) Primary School, Orwell

Me

Penny is my name
Turquoise is my colour
Running is my game
Pasta is my fave in every way
Meeting new people is nice
It is like me.

Penelope Ord (9)
Petersfield CE (A) Primary School, Orwell

My Dream For The Future!

The cute cat in the big box
Quivered in the corner looking rather lost
Then she saw a ferocious fox!
She wanted to live whatever the cost

Along came an adventurous girl,
The cat was scared of all in the world
Though the girl persevered, she wanted to help
The fox came towards the cat, she started to yelp
The girl grabbed her quickly and took her home
The cat was loved dearly, she had her own throne

A couple of years passed and the cat had kittens
Their beautiful names were Rosemary, Blossom,
and Mittens
The girl provided a secure home and welcomed
more and more
There were cats in strange places and all over the
floor
I know this girl well as this girl is me
My dream for the future is to create a happy cat
family.

Kayla-Rose Astbury (9)
Prenton Primary School, Prenton

Liam's Acrostic Poem!

L is for loving. I enjoy showing people how much I care.

I is for intelligent. I am always keen to learn.

A is for ambition. One day I wish to represent Liverpool FC.

M is for mature. I always try to support others and share my ideas.

P is for polite. I always have manners and I am respectful to others.

H is for honesty. I am always truthful.

E is for enthusiasm. Always trying my best to succeed in everything I do.

N is for never giving up!

N is nostalgic. I like to keep my memories close to my heart.

A is for adventures. I love to explore and discover new places.

H is for humour. I like to make people smile and laugh.

Liam Phennah (10)

Prenton Primary School, Prenton

What Inspired Me To Be Me?

I was inspired by my mum to write this poem
because she is my best chum -
I love my mum so much because when I've hurt
myself she has the magic touch.

I was inspired by my dad because when I'm sad, he
makes me feel glad.

I was inspired by my nan because she's my biggest
fan -
She loves to tan under the sun.

My grandad cooks the best meal I've ever had,
Mmmmm... chicken curry!

Eva, my big sister, has always got a dancing fever!

Lowri is my stepmum, she's always nice and happy.

My little sister, Arabella, loves Fruitella.

These are the reasons I love my family,
I am so lucky to have them!

Charlotte Davies (8)
Prenton Primary School, Prenton

This Is Me

My name is Amelia
This poem is about me
I live with my brothers, Connor and Harry
My mum, my dad and my cute puppy too
I like him the most, keep that to you!

I have lots of friends
Some in my school year
I see others on Fridays
When we go to cheer.

Brownies, they're so nice to eat
It's also a club
Where me and my friends meet.

I like to go swimming on Tuesdays the most
I like winning
When we do backstroke.

To be kind, helpful, loving
Is important to me
I do this every day
Just ask my family.

I hope you have learnt a bit more about me
One thing to remember
I love my family.

Amelia Tullett (8)
Prenton Primary School, Prenton

Best Days

I wake up early at the weekend, there is no lie-in for me,
But not to worry because Mum's making me an energy breakie,
She helps me get my socks on and slides my shin pads in too,
All while I'm on YouTube catching up on Bondi Rescue.

We have to leave soon, my game kicks off at 9,
I'm not nervous today and my drink is a bottle of Prime,
As I stand on the pitch as a left winger,
I'm hoping today I'll score a pinger.

The coach is my dad,
For that, I am so glad,
These are the best days, playing with my team,
One day I'll play for Tranmere and that is my dream.

Teddie Cummins (9)
Prenton Primary School, Prenton

All About Me

K ind is what I try to be
I n my life to help others
N ever will I be cruel to any
D oing fun things with my brother

F eeling happy, laughing freely
U sing jokes to have a giggle
N ever bored, always shining

S ums and numbers are the best
M aths is my fave subject
A long with science, I love to
R ead a lot, learn something new
T ry my best is what I do.

James Clark (9)
Prenton Primary School, Prenton

Ava's Magical Ingredients

A love of reading
And beautiful seeding
Making up tales
It never fails

I very much like art
And I always make a good start
I want to work in fashion
As it is my passion

I like to game
And it's always the same
Building blocks
I like it lots

I am learning to dance
And I always get the chance
With Mollie I go
And we dance to and fro

I have eight cousins
There's nearly dozens

My sister Sophia and I like to play
And we do it all day

I love doing my best you see
This is the end of my poem about me.

Ava Harrington (8)
Prenton Primary School, Prenton

Pikmin And Me!

Whilst Mum is busy in the kitchen
You'll always find me playing Pikmin.

I can play for hours,
Which gives me lots of gaming powers.

If I ever lose a Pikmin
I always take it on the chin.

Pikmin 1, 2, 3 and 4,
I've completed them all, for sure!

They call me the Pikmin Master,
Which is better than being a dirty gangster.

I pick up my games when I feel sad,
Then things don't ever seem so bad.

Sam Westerman (10)
Prenton Primary School, Prenton

All About Me

Hello, my name is Riley
Today, I am going to tell you why I'm so happy and smiley
I like to play games with a friend called James
But when I am at home, I am never alone!
There are four more to go over!

There's Dad, Mum and my brother, George
But, wait, there's another!
He's black and white, he will sneak through the night
If you're home alone, he will give you a fright!
But at home, we call him Patch, the cat!

Riley Adams (9)
Prenton Primary School, Prenton

This Is Me!

N ancy is so fancy

A mber is a great friend to me

N ikki is my funny mummy

C lean and tidy is what I want to be (most of the time)

Y ellow is my second favourite colour

H appiness for me is playing outside with friends

U nique and smart is me in school

L ove is my cousin's dog playing around with a ball

L oud and noisy, this is me!

Nancy Hull (8)

Prenton Primary School, Prenton

A Poem About Maths

Maths is like a puzzle you see,
Multiplication and division are fun for me.
Every day is like a test,
I try my hardest to do my best.
Shapes and fractions are quite cool,
And maths is taught in every school.
Doing maths makes me feel clever,
Solving sums and puzzles now and forever.
Percentages and decimals aren't so tough,
I'm a times table rock star so that's enough.

Alex Kell (9)
Prenton Primary School, Prenton

All About Jax

I love all things sweet, like chocolate and cake
They are the best things to eat
I spend a lot of time playing football outside
Sometimes I win, sometimes I lose
Computer games are fun to play
Like Fortnite, I do pretty alright
I have two dogs, Ted and Dash
They both love hugs
My sister thinks she is the boss, but that is me
Now you know about me, let's hear about you!

Jax Wilson (8)
Prenton Primary School, Prenton

A Recipe All About Me

A sprinkle of happiness
A sprinkle of joy
An ounce of knowledge
A teaspoon of love
A dash of kindness
A cup of memories

A jug of magic
A cup of sympathy
Plenty of spoonfuls of hugs and laughter that
never ends
An egg crack of smartness
And a mix of artistic things
A jug full of smiles and enjoyment
And, finally, a bowl of manners.

Aoife Tuohey (9)
Prenton Primary School, Prenton

Ingredients That Made Me

1 cup of kindness
A tablespoon of cheer
A pinch of manners
1 heap of trust
A splash of joy
1 dash of politeness
4 drops of self-esteem
A mix of art
A quarter of shyness
A whole lot of friendliness
4 teaspoons of fun
1 pint of honesty and smiles
2 drops of helpfulness
5 handfuls of caring
Serve everyone you meet.

Lily-Mae Colman (9)
Prenton Primary School, Prenton

Sporty Charlie

C lever passing is how I play football.

H appy is how I feel playing sport on a court.

A thletic and tall helps me head a ball.

R ugby and tennis are other sports I play.

L earning helps me never give up, to win a cup.

I mproving comes from my hard work and focus.

E ntertaining the crowd makes me feel proud.

Charlie Kennedy (8)
Prenton Primary School, Prenton

This Is Me...

My name is Harriet Jones
And I like to eat ice cream cones.

I have curly blonde hair and big blue eyes
And I love nothing more than a good surprise.

I can be very arty
And love a good party.

I love fun in the sun,
Sledging in the snow,
Kicking the autumn leaves,
And when spring comes, watching our flowers
grow.

Harriet Jones (8)
Prenton Primary School, Prenton

William

W is for wonderful, wild and whizz

I is for imaginative, independent and incredible

L is for logical, legendary and lightning

L is for lively, loyal and laughing

I is for invisible, impressive and ice cream

A is for active, amazing and awesome

M is for magical, marvellous and mind-blowing.

William Mellor (8)

Prenton Primary School, Prenton

All About Me

F antastic like a fox,
E xcellent like an eagle,
R esilient like a reindeer,
N ice like a narwhal.

P assionate like a penguin,
O utstanding like an otter,
W ild like a wolf,
E nergetic like an emu,
R espectful like a robin,
S tylish like a swan.

Fern Powers
Prenton Primary School, Prenton

I Like

I like to dance
And also prance
I love commercial
I practise in rehearsal
It is a mix of hip-hop and street
You need to feel a dancing beat
Attitude and a sassy move
Helps to get me in the groove
You can wear something ragged
It might be a bit jagged
You may see me prance
And I love to dance.

Aubree Wood (9)
Prenton Primary School, Prenton

What Makes Me Sad And Happy

My cat Floyd makes me happy,
He is such a funny chappy,
He's grey and big and fluffy,
He's better than a puppy,
He loves food like me.
He loves his tea.

My cat makes me feel sad,
Sometimes he is bad,
He scratches me a lot,
He is sometimes mad,
But he's still a lovely lad.

Clara Kate Eaton (10)
Prenton Primary School, Prenton

My Recipe To Make Me!

300g of smiles
5 piles of kindness
7 tablespoons of cuteness
8lbs pounds of craziness
12 litres of thoughtfulness
A pinch of madness
A handful of hungriness

Mix it all together in a bowl and put it in the oven
for only two minutes...
Because I'm impatient!

Elsie McEwan (9)
Prenton Primary School, Prenton

Doggy Poem

Running in the garden, me and Simon play,
Chasing each other, having fun all day.
When Dad comes home, Simon takes flight.
Excitement in his eyes, his tail wags with delight.
Simon, he's a silly dog, he always brings smiles.
With antics and playfulness that go on for miles.

Abel Hassall (8)
Prenton Primary School, Prenton

When I'm Older

I wish I had a turtle
I would probably call him Myrtle
I wouldn't paint it purple.

I like to run
I find it really fun.

I want to be a doctor
But not a pimple popper.

I would rather fix knees
Because they don't smell like cheese.

Lily Jones (9)
Prenton Primary School, Prenton

All About Me

I am tall,
I am sporty,
As fast as a lightning bolt.
I eat a lot,
I move a lot,
And on the trampoline, I can do a somersault.
I am kind,
I am smart,
And I help others too.
I am fun,
And I am loud,
So tell me,
Who are you?

Luca Turaga (10)
Prenton Primary School, Prenton

I Am Smart

S is for sharing, which I do with my friends
M is for Mason, which is my first name
A is for artistic, because I like to create drawings
R is for reading, which I do every night
T is for tutor, who I see every Tuesday.

Mason Millet (9)
Prenton Primary School, Prenton

Tennis

T ennis makes me happy
E very day I'd love to play
N othing can stop me from playing
N ever in a mood to not play the brilliant game
I want to play at Wimbledon
S o I'd better keep practising.

Pascal Pierre-Louis (8)
Prenton Primary School, Prenton

Tilly's Poem

I am Tilly
I am fun
I am caring
And I like to be in the sun

I love Stitch
I love ice cream
I want to be rich
But I can dream

I am Tilly
I am nice
I can be silly
But I can give advice.

Tilly Fletcher (9)
Prenton Primary School, Prenton

This Is Me - Jessica

Jessica is an ordinary girl who is kind and likes to play football. This is me.

J olly and joyful
E nthusiastic
S uperb
S ensible
I nquisitive
C reative
A dorable.

Jessica Edwards (8)
Prenton Primary School, Prenton

Ella

E ach and every day I look for new adventure
L ove building dens in the park
L aughing, chatting and enjoying my new venture
A fterwards having an ice cream, enjoying my
quiet time and listening to the lark.

Ella Thomason (8)

Prenton Primary School, Prenton

Dance, Dance, Dance

Dance, dance, dance the night away
I could do it every day
I like to dance in my own way
Top rocks and six steps all the way
Dancing on stage is so much fun
Crowd cheering at the stage
I'm very good at my age.

Osian Pollard (8)
Prenton Primary School, Prenton

What Ingredients Make Me

A box of kindness, cuddles too,
2 jugs of funniness and more too
A handful of smartness
4 is 2+2
A squeeze of friendship
And last but not least
Add a bit of sadness
Which isn't true
Thanks to you.

Isla Carroll (10)
Prenton Primary School, Prenton

All About Me

G ood

E nergetic

O rganised

R esponsible

G enerous

E asy-going

S porty

A dventurous

N ice

D elightful

S trong.

George Sands (9)

Prenton Primary School, Prenton

Your Friend Harry!

H appiness is my favourite feeling.
A cting and laughter I find most healing.
R ugby is my favourite sport.
R espect and kindness I have been taught.
Y our friend Harry.

Harry Hogan (8)
Prenton Primary School, Prenton

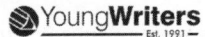

Doggie Dottie

My little doggie Dottie
I love you very much
She's small and brown with pointed ears
She jumps high for a treat
Which makes me smile
I love my little doggie Dottie.

Annabel Shields (9)
Prenton Primary School, Prenton

All About Me

S uper

U nbelievable

M agnificent

M agnificent

E xcellent

R esilient

L oving

I ndependent.

Summer Li (9)

Prenton Primary School, Prenton

This Is Ella

This is me, happy, cheery, sad and angry.
This is me, green eyes, brown hair, beige skin.
This is me, knitting, reading, playing games.
I am me and no one else is.

Ella Grant (8)
Prenton Primary School, Prenton

Under The Big Top

A mazing Amber spinning in the air
M onkeys climbing everywhere
B ig and small, no fear at all
E lephant, dancing tigers
R oar!

Amber Doyle (8)
Prenton Primary School, Prenton

Football Lover

James is football-mad, he loves to watch Tranmere
Even when they lose and it makes him sad
James is creative, clever and fun
His helpful nature gets the job done.

James Malloy (10)

Prenton Primary School, Prenton

Jolly Times

There was a boy called Ollie
Who was always fun and jolly
He loved to play chaos tag
But always seemed to lose his rag
And then all his mum would do is nag.

Oliver McNicholas (9)
Prenton Primary School, Prenton

Doggies

I have a dog, he is very cheeky,
He has lots of toys, his favourite is squeaky.
He likes his treats and sleeps on my bed,
I like to pat his little soft head.

Jude Wynne (9)
Prenton Primary School, Prenton

A Sprinkle Of Me

In a cauldron goes a spoonful of happiness
A dash of imagination
A sprinkle of laughter
A handful of fun
A bit of sport
That is what makes me.

Isaac Arch (9)
Prenton Primary School, Prenton

Ava

My name is Ava
I'm active
I'm Ava
I'm very happy
My name is Ava
I'm amazing.

Ava Critchley (9)
Prenton Primary School, Prenton

Harry's Acrostic Poem

H ard-working
A thletic
R esilient
R espectful
Y our friend.

Harry Hargreaves (10)
Prenton Primary School, Prenton

Happiness

A pinch of kind
A sprinkle of fun
A boom of happiness
And that is what makes a human kind.

Lyla Finnigan (9)
Prenton Primary School, Prenton

All About Me!

O ptimistic

S mart

C alm

A dventurous

R esilient.

Oscar McCarthy-Gordon (9)
Prenton Primary School, Prenton

All About Me

I am kind,
I am smart.
I like hearts.
I am part of life just like you!

Alexandra Harris (9)
Prenton Primary School, Prenton

This Is Me

I am happy sometimes and I am sporty,
I have brown hair but my teacher's is long and
shiny.
I have four cats but I also like dogs,
I have lots of money and I am very funny.
I am kind and I can also find,
I have long hair but I want it short and spiky.
We all have different colour eyes but mine are
brown,
We all have different colour hair but mine is brown,
And sometimes I frown.
I wish to be rich but where is the switch?
I am kind, helpful and funny, but so is my teacher.
I have brown, fluffy hair that flows in the wind,
My dark brown eyes are like melted chocolate,
I am as tall as a bear,
This is me.

Theodore Jeyes (9)
Wombridge Primary School, Oakengates

I'm Perfectly Fine Because...

I'm perfectly fine because I have unique, curly hair, waving to the air.
I have perfect dark eyes as sharp as a spy.
I have soft glossy lips as reflective as clear water.
I'm so tall I can reach the top shelf.
I'm so fit that people just assume I go to the gym.

I'm perfectly fine because I'm as intelligent as a mobile calculator.
I'll answer anything you ask, you'll be surprised.

I'm as responsible as a brave lioness who is protective over her child.
I'm so funny you can't compare me to anything.
I'm so kind I wouldn't hurt a fly and I wouldn't miss one goodbye.

I'm perfectly fine because when I grow up I want to be a footballer as a profession.
But this is no ordinary confession.
For I will face no distraction.

When I retire I'll go to university to study medicine.
I'll become a doctor until I'm too old to work.
And when I'm all done I'll travel to New York.
I want to be inspiring, to get children's spirits firing.

Angel Ofori (9)
Wombridge Primary School, Oakengates

About My Day

I want to make a poem
To tell you about my day
When all the parents came to class
You had to stay away.

We did a spot of maths
A dash of English too
A slice (and more) of reading
I'd like to read to you.

I felt a handful of sadness
And had a flake of love
I started to feel gloomy
But I knew it was above.

I swallowed a glug of bravery
Because I knew just what to do
When I got home with my family
I'd serve it up to you.

A whisk-up of my good day
And all that happened there

With doodles of fun I had
With you I had to share

I'm thankful you can be with me
On this lovely and fine day
I get to share it after school
I'm pleased I'm on my way

Home is noisy, home is fun
It's what I like best
School is enjoyable, work is hard
But I can tell you the rest.

Austin Booth (10)
Wombridge Primary School, Oakengates

How To Make Me!

How to make your own Samuella,
These are step-by-step instructions,
So follow carefully!

First add half a cup of appreciation,
Then add two spoons of humble tears,
Balance it out with three spoons of happiness.

Mix in a cup of kindness, with a spoon of funniness,
Knead until just right,
Then incorporate it with the dough.

Add a few drops of enthusiasm,
And two cups of friendliness,
Then whisk until the dough is not blotchy in colour.

Add in my love for art,
And four scoops of creativity,
Bake for just one minute.

Take it out and infuse it with oxygen,
Shape it into a human.

Put it back in the oven and bake until you hear a...
Boom!
Well done you have made your Samuella.

All you need to do now is catch her,
Good luck!

Samuella Boateng (11)
Wombridge Primary School, Oakengates

I Am Me!

I am very generous and kind!
A super-fast mind like Sonic the Hedgehog
We have different hair colour but mine is gold,
My gold hair has the shiniest flair!
I am me.

I am Bay, I'm funny all day!
I have a contagious smile and I will make you laugh,
Go trick or treating at my door,
You might be afraid of my mighty roar!
I'm sweet, I'm sour, I will make you cower,
I am playful, I am fun,
I am Bay and I was born in May!
I am me.

I am smart, so I am a star!
I am rich, I am secretly a witch!
I want to be a Starbucks worker,
So at the end of my shift,
I can get the latest drinks,
I am me.

I am brave,
I am bored,
I am deflated,
I am surprised,
I am hurt,
I am proud,
I am friendly,
I am a rainbow of emotions,
I am me!

Bay Toro Pearce (9)
Wombridge Primary School, Oakengates

I Am Me!

Here are some instructions,
To be myself,
I can be who I want to be,
And I don't need to listen to anyone else.

To start add a dash of confidence,
To show who you really are,
Then take a sprinkle of enthusiasm,
And a smile will get you far.

Add a handful of courageousness,
To help people when they need it,
Make sure to add a slice of kindness,
So then you can be an example to everyone -
believe it!

Now make sure to scatter some sympathy on top,
To stand up to people if you need to,
Finally, sprinkle on some optimism,
To look forward in bad situations around you.

Make sure you don't let anyone drag you down,
You don't need to change for anyone,

You are perfect just the way you are,
Always remember that fact for everyone!

Eleya-Sky Sandhu (11)
Wombridge Primary School, Oakengates

Who I Am

My eyes are brown and round
When I look into the mirror
They will always make me
Feel different and sweet.

I'm short, not tall
I can fit into tiny holes
And win games of hide-and-seek.

My dark brown hair is special to me
When it blows in the calming wind
It blows and I feel like an amazing superstar.

Who I am

I'm kind and sweet and
That's all I need to be.

I'm friendly and funny
I can always put a smile on anyone's face.

I'm positive and try something new
No matter what.

I may be tiny but this is what
Makes me truly who I am.

Who I am

I wish I could be a vet
And save animals every day
And let them truly
Be who they are.

Anka Yuen (9)
Wombridge Primary School, Oakengates

This Is Me!

I am beautiful as my mum calls me beautiful every day,
I have green eyes as they shine like emeralds,
I have long blonde hair as it shines in the sun,

I am happy when I have sweets but not when I hear beats,
I am clever and kind, you can call me Mrs Einstein,
I am sporty and love football but hate netball,
I like animals but hate flannels,
I am sweet or sour depending on the hour,

I am rich but secretly a witch,
Witches cast spells but I cast bells,

I am shy,
I am scared,
I am happy,
I am hurt,
I am brave,
I am a variety of emotions,

I laugh when my dog runs around the house like a lunatic,
But I'm not laughing when she breaks all my stuff,

This is me!

Alice Figura (9)
Wombridge Primary School, Oakengates

The Perfect Me

This is a list of ingredients,
To create what stuff makes me,
Show everybody how to be yourself,
And mash up my character and personality.

To start we need a splash of energy,
Plus a drizzle of determination makes me my best,
Add a colossal splash of sports,
Then saute some football, of which I never rest.

Now whisk in plenty of optimism,
A teaspoon of self-esteem,
Boil with caring,
But keep me nice and clean.

Next a glug of tiredness,
And shake it all around,
A pinch of weights and workouts,
And don't forget sick sounds.

Simmer it with math-making,
After, serve me perfectly,

Decorate with carefulness,
I'm a real delight to see.

Zaiden Christie-Lewis (10)
Wombridge Primary School, Oakengates

What Makes Me

Here are some instructions
To make me, me
They make up my feelings
And my personality.

First add a slice of gratefulness,
A pinch of positivity will be fine,
Then a handful of adventurousness,
And a dab of awkwardness follows behind.

Now whip in lots of sportiness,
Add a hint of stupidity,
Then a chunk of crushed madness
And whisk it all up just for me.

Put it in a pan,
Sprinkle a bit of anxiousness,
Then add a bit of intelligence,
And pour a dollop of confidence.

Cook it right, boil or bake,
Then decorate me so bold,

Glaze with a drizzle of cheerfulness,
As I'm a real delight to behold.

Millie Summers (11)
Wombridge Primary School, Oakengates

The Best Version Of Me

I'm sporty and fun,
When it comes to football.
I'm grumpy as a bottle,
When people get wise.
I'm as quiet as a mouse,
But when it comes to English,
I'm as loud as a lion.

When it comes to basketball,
That's where I shine.
I won't give up on my dream,
Because my friends are with me.
I'm okay with reading,
Some days are good,
Some days are bad,
But I never give up.

My favourite songs are usually rock songs,
When I listen to rock, my body goes *pop*.
The person who inspired me is my new teacher
Miss Simkin,

Now I'm brave, strong and unique.
I'm not afraid to be me!

Yusra Durmaz (9)
Wombridge Primary School, Oakengates

Me, Myself And I

My name is Bella,
My favourite colour is yellow,
My favourite sweet is a marshmallow,
That's me.

My BFF's name is Daisy
My doll's name is Maisie
But my doll's a bit crazy
That's me

My favourite character is Hermione
My least favourite character is Bellatrix
My second favourite is Hagrid
That's me

My hair is like a brown bear
It is scary to untangle
My bear hair is nice when it's done right
That's me

My favourite character is Stitch
But I do not like the situation

My dream is to be a rich artist someday
That's me.

Isabella Lane (9)
Wombridge Primary School, Oakengates

This Is Me

We all have different hair, I have mixed,
Mine is brown and blonde,
I love my hair because it's nice and soft,
I have blue eyes like the sea,
I speak Polish all the time,
I'm 156cm tall,
I'm fit and healthy and not heavy.

I'm funny and arty,
I like to play football all the time,
My hobby is fishing, I do not know why,
I'm as fast as a cheetah,
I plan to be a pro footballer,
I like Harry Potter and I like nature,
I'm not rich but I am grateful for all the things I have.

I want to be famous and rich,
And have a lot of pets.
Nobody is going to stop me.

Natan Jeszke (9)
Wombridge Primary School, Oakengates

What Makes Me Be Me

Here are some instructions,
To create what makes me be me,
They combine to make my character,
And my personality.

First take a chunk of awkwardness,
Then a tad of positivity,
A huge drop of happiness,
And a dash of kindness works best.

Now whisk in loads of caringness,
Add a teaspoon of self-doubt,
Now put it in a blender,
And shake it all about.

And now add a hint of shyness,
Add a pinch of adventurousness,
Take a dollop of joy,
And mix it all up.

Now serve me up just right,
Decorate me with anxiousness,
As I'm a real delight.

Heather Cope (10)
Wombridge Primary School, Oakengates

I Am Me

I am smart,
I am kind,
I am everything,
I am me.

My glasses are my life,
Without them, I am blind,
I am me.

You can call me Einstein's brother,
I am not really bothered,
I love being myself,
I am me.

I wish for a family,
Hopefully, I'll still be happy,
I am me.

I love school,
But when French comes, I'd rather cower,
I enjoy learning,
I am me.

Palaeontology is my power,
I adore science,
I am me.

My hazel eyes,
And brown hair,
Don't make me different,
I don't care,
I am me.

Ksawery Borowski (10)
Wombridge Primary School, Oakengates

I Am Beautiful

I am beautiful

My fabulous sky-blue
Eyes are like ocean waves splashing on a beach
My blonde hair is as yellow as a beach
Drawing with yellow sand

I am beautiful

I am funny and all
But I am cool
I am smart as a scientist
But I don't want to be as tiny

I am most caring but when I'm older
I will be wearing a business suit for my job

I am beautiful
I want to be a dad but dads are usually mad
So I don't want to be that kind of dad

I want to have the most happy family in existence
I want to be happy like a happy emoji!

Harley Peters (9)
Wombridge Primary School, Oakengates

208

How To Make Me

Take a look at this recipe,
To make a perfect me,
Follow each instruction,
And measure carefully.

First take a gallon of sporty juice,
Then a slice of funniness,
A huge dollop of happy vibes,
And a drizzle of caring works best.

Now whisk in lots of football skills,
Add a teaspoon of optimism too,
Add in a tipple of self-doubt,
Then mixing together is what you do.

Now pour in a gallon of confidence,
Then add five teaspoons of smartness too,
And finally add a trickle of passion,
And shake it all about,
And there you go, you made your own Jakub!

Jakub Florkiewicz (10)
Wombridge Primary School, Oakengates

How To Make Me Be Me!

Please read carefully
Because this is how to make Michealangelo (me)
And this is the only mixture available.

First add a slice of unexpected emotions
After make a jolly mash of football skills
Then a mixture of happiness
Then a stir of loveliness.

After mix a bit of sportiness
And a thimbleful of funniness
Then a pinch of positivity
After add a mix of cluelessness.

Whisk in a dab of astonishment
Next pour in a drip of drippiness
Simmer it with friendliness
And try not to make a mess.

And *boom!* You have your own Michealangelo.

Michealangelo Okeke (11)
Wombridge Primary School, Oakengates

Sophie's Recipe

What you need to make me:
Two big sprinkles of smile powder,
A sprinkle of mischief,
A whole tablespoon of hair,
A bowl of kindness,
Three tablespoons of loveliness,
Two spoons of respect,
A cup of basketball,
Four spoons of gaming.

Now:
1. Start by mixing a cup of basketball with your spoons of gaming.
2. Once it's full of mischief, add three tablespoons of respect and two spoons of loveliness into a bowl of kindness.
3. Lay the mixture on a tablespoon of hair.
4. Once bubbling with mischief, sprinkle smile powder on top.

Thank you for creating me!

Sophie Farley
Wombridge Primary School, Oakengates

Things That Make Me!

My big brown eyes make my mum say, "Beautiful."
I like wearing shorts and I like sports.
I am kind and I have a mathematician's mind.
I hate school but I like going in the pool.
My speedy run makes me go all bleedy.
I love football but sometimes my team loses.

I love dogs but I don't like doves.
My books make me enjoy reading,
And I took a good book.
People like baths but I like maths.
I am funny at being a funny bunny.

I wish to be rich but not a snitchy witch.
I like my voice but not the noise.
My skills are great but not always.

Alfie Cruise (9)
Wombridge Primary School, Oakengates

All About Me

All about me
A zebra is as tall as me but he is as thin as a slide
so we don't match.
My arms are tanned because the sun shines on
them.
My dusty blonde hair is as straight as a noodle in
your soup.

All about me
I'm brave like a penguin catching fish in the dark,
deep ocean.
I'm perfect like a Pringle and single like a Pringle.
My perfect kind teacher makes me never give up.

All about me
I want to be a famous artist like Miss Jones.
If I'm an actor I want to be like Jenna Ortega.
I'm flexible like a noodle so I could join the
Olympics.

Zoe Gyorfi (9)
Wombridge Primary School, Oakengates

How To Make Me

Here is a list of ingredients,
Of what you need to make me,
Combine them together with love and care,
To create my personality.

First sprinkle a tad of funniness,
Then add a slice of caring too,
Drop a hint of craziness in the mix,
And make a paste is what you do.

Now blend in a glug of kindness,
Then three teaspoons of determination and sass,
Please supplement me with confidence,
So that I stand out in my class.

Next add a bit of sarcasm,
And a blob of joyful glee,
Decorate with daring,
I'm Amber and this is me!

Amber-Rose Mancini (11)
Wombridge Primary School, Oakengates

What Makes Me Be Me

Here are some instructions,
To create a potion of me,
If you listen carefully you will,
Get a taste of my personality.

First take a slice of happiness,
Then a dab of laughter,
A huge handful of confidence,
And a smattering of sportiness,
Works best.

Now whisk in lots of competitiveness,
Add a tablespoon of ambition,
Then mix it and mix it,
And shake it all about.

To finish it off,
Sprinkle in some eagerness,
Then a drizzle of peacefulness,
Decorate with musicality,
And I'm a real delight.

Layla Shaw
Wombridge Primary School, Oakengates

The Secret Ingredient

Here is a secret ingredient,
To create what makes me, me,
They combine my personality,
And my character you see.

First take a gallon of gloominess,
Then a pennyworth of frustration,
A huge chipping of courageousness,
And a chunk of artwork, best for this creation.

Now whisk in lots of enthusiasm,
Add a fraction of humour and tricks,
Infuse it all in optimism,
And shake it all about to mix.

Add a handful of horse riding,
Then serve me up alright,
Decorate with elegance,
Almost perfect, but not quite!

Tawny Toro-Pearce (10)
Wombridge Primary School, Oakengates

The Recipe To Me!

Here are the instructions,
To create my personality,
Follow them carefully,
Or it could turn out tragically.

First add a large slice of caring,
A large dollop of friendship,
Whisk in some self-doubt,
Add a drizzle of humour to the tip.

Now whisk in some fear,
And a teaspoon of creativeness,
Stir, stir, stir up this delight,
And don't make a mess!

Add some happiness-flavoured sprinkles,
And buttons of enthusiasm for me,
But sometimes the taste won't show,
Now enjoy a tasty recipe!

Georgia Jackson (11)
Wombridge Primary School, Oakengates

This Is Me!

I love my dark brown hair
Because it shines as bright as the sun
You should call me special
Because I brighten up everyone's faces
Sometimes I'm happy, sometimes I'm sad
It just depends on the sour hour
I love cats, but you might not
But we can still be friends
Go trick or treating and knock on my door
Run because you will be scared of my horrible roar
This is me!

I am happy, I am sour
It just depends on the hour
I like Stitch but I hate a witch
I am as brave as a wildcat
This is me!

Anita Chozhgova (9)
Wombridge Primary School, Oakengates

My Name Is Izzy

I am amazing in my own way because I am a
reader,
And I like to play,
I sneak into school to go to the library,
I love to read all of the books.

Sometimes when I am not very careful I get caught
by the adults,
I always talk to myself, so I'm easy to catch you
see.

I'm only nine, but I look twelve, I love myself the
way I am,
I still need to work on getting braver and stronger,
If you ever fail keep trying like me and never give
up as soon as you think you should,
This is me and I'm as proud as I can be.

Izobelle Birnbaum (9)
Wombridge Primary School, Oakengates

This Is Me

This is me,
You may have blonde or red hair but I have brown,
If you're friends with me, you'll never frown.
You may have long hair but I have short,
I love playing sport.
I love cats and dogs but prefer cats,
If you don't agree, you're better than that.
I am funny, I am kind,
But dislike mimes.
I want to become a police officer,
To protect me from crime,
If I don't, I'll feel like slime.
To be my friend, just ask,
If I ask you to do something,
It's a very simple task.

Nicole Marsh (9)
Wombridge Primary School, Oakengates

This Is Me!

I am happy,
Lovely grins all around,
I'd love to spend my pocket money, just a pound!
Now I go to school, it's so fun,
When I play, I go on a long run.

I am hyper,
Eating sweets with loads of sugar,
I've gone crazy, now I'm a runner!
The silliness, that's not good,
I cannot learn, or I could.

I am jealous,
It's not fair, I'll take that,
Give that to me, it's a beautiful cat!
No manners, just too rude,
Just hungry, I want to eat all the food.

Tyrese Mancini (8)
Wombridge Primary School, Oakengates

I Am Me

We all have different colour hair, mine is brown,
Sometimes I have a frown,
I have a superpower, it's to be kind and helpful,
My eyes are brown and I can see down.

I love to do cartwheels,
So watch me spin,
I'm kind and confident,
I love dogs but I hate frogs,
I don't like ties but I love pies.

Watch me spin doing cartwheels,
I hope to be a gymnast,
I'm not good at crafts, I guarantee
All my friends are better than me,
I am rich and I love Stitch.

Daisy Roberts (9)
Wombridge Primary School, Oakengates

What Makes Me Be Me

Here are some instructions,
To create what makes me be me.
They combine my character,
And my personality.

First bake a handful of positiveness,
And a slice of gratefulness.
A huge glug of joy,
And an ounce of fearless works best.

Now whisk in lots of happiness,
Add a sprinkle of self-doubt.
Dab it all in shyness,
And shake it all about.

Simmer it with thrilled-ness,
Then serve me up just right,
Decorate with elegance,
As I'm a real delight.

Lucia Woodrow (10)
Wombridge Primary School, Oakengates

This Is Me

I'm as sweet as pie
My hair is blonde and brown
Sometimes I frown
I wish to be a star, so I become smart
I'm a good friend and I like to dance

I wish to be a designer like Cruella de Vil
I'm fantastic like Bey, even know she slays all day
I want to be a Starbucks worker so I get free drinks
I wish to be famous like Lisa from Blackpink

I'm happy
I'm sad
I like to smile
I like to frown
Hi, I'm Sydney
I love Stitch, he's my heart.

Sydney Keen (9)
Wombridge Primary School, Oakengates

What Makes Me Be Me

Here are some instructions
To create what makes me,
These add to my character,
And all that makes me happy.

First take a pinch of caring,
Then a grating of love works best,
A huge dollop of humour,
And a flake of handsomeness.

Then a glug of optimism,
A huge gallon of care,
A thimbleful of cleverness,
I think we're almost there.

Now mix in an ounce of fishermen,
A fraction of braveness too,
A tad of positivity,
To make the perfect stew.

Riley Locker (11)
Wombridge Primary School, Oakengates

What Makes Me Be Me

Here are some instructions
To create what makes me, me.
They combine to make my character
And my personality.

First take a sprinkle of jolly,
Then a whisk of adventurous,
A huge flake of kindness
And a slice of bravery works best.

Now add a trace of shyness,
Add a gallon of bitter,
Infuse it all in confidence
And shake it all about.

Chunk it with cleanliness
Then serve me up just right.
Decorate me with courage,
I'm a real delight!

Emilija Stikovaite (10)
Wombridge Primary School, Oakengates

What Makes Me

Here is a lovely recipe,
To create what makes me, me.
They combine to form my character,
And creates what you see.

First take a slice of appreciation,
Then a pinch of glee.
Scatter it in excitement,
Add a drizzle of love from me.

Now whisk in lots of intelligence,
Add a teaspoon of self-doubt.
Then a tad of stupidity,
And shake it all about.

Add a hint of shyness,
Stir me up all day.
Decorate with elegance,
You've made a Lillymae!

Lillymae Hoey (10)
Wombridge Primary School, Oakengates

This Is Me!

How to make me,
The recipe for my character,
And my funny personality.

First, add a gallon of kindness,
Then a pinch of helpfulness,
A sprinkle of independence,
Then a scoop of positivity.

A twinkle of sportiness,
Then add a dollop of dance,
A slice of sassiness,
Then a pinch of braveness.

A slab of a growth mindset,
Now add 10lb of good listening,
Then add a sprinkle of happiness,
And ten grams of mischief.

This is me!

Larissa Arnold (11)
Wombridge Primary School, Oakengates

The Interesting Recipe For Me!

Follow the instructions,
Then you'll get me,
They mix together nicely,
And they're very simple and easy!

A gallon of humour,
A tidbit of fear,
Add a truckload of cleverness,
Then whisk for eleven years.

A tad of daring,
A teaspoon of optimism,
A dollop of getting muddy,
Then place it in the oven!

Sprinkle on some love,
Drizzle on some pride,
Serve with a dish of farming,
And the mechanics will be just right!

James Farley (11)
Wombridge Primary School, Oakengates

What Makes Me, Me!

I live my life in style
What's more important is my smile

I mix some comedy with laughter, a drop of
craziness is all you need
I'm always happy, how do you plead?

My sportiness is what I have in my bag
I don't mean to nag

I sprinkle some paint with a paintbrush
I mix it all together and make art

My heart is as warm as a radiator, I like my space
With a bit of helpfulness, sometimes I need a break

This is me!

Stephen Smith (11)
Wombridge Primary School, Oakengates

What Makes Me Be Me

First take a slice of humour,
Then a pinch of kindness
And a huge chunk of positive
And a touch of thankfulness.

Now spot in lots of cheerful,
Add a handful of fearless,
Flake it all into colourfulness
And chipping it all about.

Now add a piece of helpless and hopeful,
Add some confidence and bravery,
Add a gallon of shyness,
A scattering of laughter.
Add a scrap of shockingness,
A dab of happiness and a drizzle of hard work.

Cho San (Kevis) Lam (10)
Wombridge Primary School, Oakengates

What's Special About Me?

I love me.
My hair is as dark as chocolate.
My eyes are memorable,
As they shimmer like the blue ocean.
My freckles are brown, little,
And light up my face like the sun.
I love me.
I am mostly kind like a unicorn,
But I can turn into a rhino.
My personality is great,
But it can get better with a flick of a switch.
I am as smart as a scientist.
I love me.
My worldwide dream is to be a rugby captain.
I'm as strong as King Kong.

Imogen Martin (9)
Wombridge Primary School, Oakengates

A Poem About Myself

I'm as tall as a giraffe,
Amazing at maths,
I have bushy, brown hair,
That shimmers and shines in the sun,
I'm always happy,
But sometimes snappy.

I like reading,
But not at all sleeping,
Of course, I like games,
But sometimes they make me angry,
Like fiery flames.

I want to be a professional hockey player,
Playing in the good weather,
And I want to be really famous,
This is everything about myself.

Connor Godwin (9)
Wombridge Primary School, Oakengates

What Makes Me Be Me

How to make your very own Shannon,
Follow my step-by-step instructions,
They combine for my character,
And my personality.

First take a hint of enthusiasm,
Then an ounce of optimism,
A large dollop of caring,
And a drizzle of humour works best.

Now stir in lots of happiness,
Add a dash of confidence,
Infuse it all in positivity,
And shake with determination.

Simmer it with shyness,
Then serve me up just right,
Finish it off with a sprinkle of eager,
Remember I'm always polite!

Shannon Dorricott (10)
Wombridge Primary School, Oakengates

This Is Me

Follow this recipe to get the perfect me -

First combine a teaspoon of loyalty,
With a dash of independence,
A gallon of being girly,
And a slice of sass.

Now mix in a pinch of being a people pleaser,
Followed by a scoop of happiness,
A drizzle of Taylor Swift fan,
And a trickle of craziness.

Then add in a dollop of optimism,
And give it a good whisk.

This is the best way to describe me.

Karina Nedeloiu (11)
Wombridge Primary School, Oakengates

What Makes Me, Me!

To create me you will need:
A drop of honesty
A pinch of craziness
A messy room full of clothes
A sprinkle of chattiness
A slab of sassiness
A room full of my dog's cuddles.

Now you need to:
Add 10lb of sass
Now a messy room full of clothes
Stir roughly for a while, adding a messy room
Next add a hot slab of chattiness
Then add a drizzle of rudeness
A slab of competitiveness and a hint of gold.

Destiny Lamb (10)
Wombridge Primary School, Oakengates

The Special Things About Me

The special things about me.

As I walk outside to see the stunning sky,
I lie down and my amazing eyes glisten through
the sun.
My tall, long legs help me to be as strong as Hulk.

The special things about me.

I'm caring, I'm kind.
I'm positive, I'm friendly,
But when someone is mean I can break it up and
be a bit sassy.

I wish to be a spectacular dancer and I can dance
with my friends.

Mary Nelson (10)
Wombridge Primary School, Oakengates

All About Me

All about me
My hair is really pretty and it is dark blonde,
My eyes are as blue as the ocean waves,
I am as small as a hamster.

All about me
I am as smart as a teacher,
I am as strong as a bear,
I am super sassy and also super caring,
I am super friendly like a dog.

All about me
I wish I was an Olympic gymnast,
I want to be better at it,
I hope to be a singer like Billie Eilish.

Olivia Hayes (9)

Wombridge Primary School, Oakengates

This Is Me

We are all different,
But I wear shorts and I'm sporty.
My superpower is maths,
But spelling tests make me jump.

I am kind and happy,
But when it rains, my smile goes away.
I am sad sometimes,
But when you give me sweets, it makes me smile.

I love football but hate tennis,
When I get a goal, I shoot away.
My feet run as fast as lightning,
This is who I want to be.

Isabelle Jones (9)
Wombridge Primary School, Oakengates

This Is Me

I'm a handful of love
And a dollop of kindness
I love creating stories
If you want to create me you need
A sprinkle of art
A flake of adventurous
A dab of sweetness
A speck of magic
To that place far away is where you will find me
I'm an ounce of braveness
A pinch of happiness
You have found the mixture you need
Now stir with elegance
And kindness you see.

Kaylen Thomas (10)
Wombridge Primary School, Oakengates

To Create Me You Will Need

To create me you will need:
A hint of humour,
A side of kindness,
A pinch of determination,
A spread of patience.
Mix in the helpfulness,
Now you will need to add a slice of kindness,
Stir in a hint of humour.
Next add a pinch, spreading some patience.
Finally, mix in the helpfulness.
Cook until golden brown,
Sprinkle on some happiness,
Then you will have baked me!

Jaycob Moore (10)
Wombridge Primary School, Oakengates

I Am Who I Am

A kennings poem

I am a...
Picky eater,
Nature lover,
Animal lover,
Fruit lover,
Science lover,
Gymnastics lover,
Dance lover,
YouTube lover,
Good wave jumper,
Early riser,
Sleep hater,
Summer wisher,
Snow wisher,
Baking lover,
Dog lover,
Computing lover,
Kind worder,
Sour lover,
Book lover,

Morning lover,
Christmas lover.

Nicola Florkiewicz (8)
Wombridge Primary School, Oakengates

This Is Me

My name is Harvey, I hate school
I like it when the bell rings
Because I get to see my dogs
I love dogs, but hate frogs

I have brown eyes and I don't like pies
We have different colour hair
Mine is brown
And most of the time, I have a frown

I wish to be a great gamer
My fingers moving like a cheetah
Through the desert
Across the keyboard.

Harvey Cartledge (9)
Wombridge Primary School, Oakengates

What Makes Me Be Me!

First take a slice of humour,
Then take a gallon of kindness,
A huge chunk of excitement,
And a gallon of happiness.

Now whisk in a lot of gratefulness,
Add in a drip of blessed,
Infuse it all up in optimism,
And shake it all about.

Simmer it with flustered-ness,
Then serve me up just right,
Decorate with elegance,
As I'm a real delight.

Mollie Sturmey (10)
Wombridge Primary School, Oakengates

The Mix Of Me

A pinch of basketball
A spoon of gaming
A piece of a burger
A teaspoon of speed
A pinch of happiness
10lb of fun and party

Now you need:
Now add a spoon of gaming
And 10lb of fun and party
A teaspoon of speed and basketball
And a pinch of happiness
Mix it all together in one
Put it in the oven until it's soft.

This is me!

Daniel Barry (9)
Wombridge Primary School, Oakengates

The Me Poem

A kennings poem

I am a...
Bike rider,
Lovely singer,
Kind lover,
Amazing baker,
Beautiful drawer,
Fast runner,
Fast swimmer,
Great dancer,
Animal lover,
Book lover,
Deep sleeper,
Good helper,
Kind helper,
Book reader,
Summer lover,
Winter lover,
Sister lover,
Me lover,
Just be you.

Kiera-Rose Sandhu (8)
Wombridge Primary School, Oakengates

What Makes Me Be Me

A dash of smartness for salt
A hit of strength as the oil.

Now add a dollop of messiness
But sprinkle a bit of good listening.

Now mix in a bit of loving to colour
But hey, you can't go wrong with a pinch of
kindness.

Wait ten minutes, then dip it into loving to game
And spread a bit of helpfulness.

Nathen Corbishley (11)
Wombridge Primary School, Oakengates

I Am Who I Am

A kennings poem

I am me...
A great bike rider,
Chocolate eater,
Roblox gamer,
Wave jumper,
Tired sleeper,
Energetic player,
Pro gamer,
Horror movie watcher,
Messy eater,
Fast runner,
Loud laugher,
Easy laugher,
Picky eater,
Slow eater,
Macaroni cooker,
This is my perfect personality.

Ana-Maria Olteanu (8)
Wombridge Primary School, Oakengates

I Love My Appearance

My hair is brown as chocolate and the blonde stripes shine in the sun.

My eyes are emerald green and shiny.

I love my appearance, such as my hair and my eyes, and how I'm kind and caring, and my personality.

When I grow up I want to be a cheer coach, because I want to be able to do all the flips and teach people how to cheer.

Ariana Corbett (9)

Wombridge Primary School, Oakengates

What Makes Me Be Me

Here are some instructions,
To create what makes me, me,
They combine for my character,
And my personality.

First take a sprinkle of confidence,
Then a handful of gratefulness,
A huge trickle of fearless,
And a gallon of eager works best.

Now drip in lots of positive,
Add a touch of hope,
Infuse it all in optimism,
And shake it all about.

Wincy Ho (11)
Wombridge Primary School, Oakengates

Life With Me

I am sweet and kind,
I am an artist,
I am a Trinidad citizen,
I am friendly,
My name is Rebekah.

Rugby is my jam,
Being fast is me,
But I am a cat,
Because I'm always sleepy,
My eyes are like dark chocolate,
My hair is a black hole,
Music is my life,
Kickboxing is self-defence,
This is me!

Rebekah Watts (9)
Wombridge Primary School, Oakengates

A Recipe For Jessica

First, gather kindness and cheerfulness,
Stir in hot, crunchy fries and pizza,
Season with paddling in a clear, sparkling pool,
Add a pinch of happy, calm music,
And watching magical fantasy movies,
Pour on acting at theatre club,
Mix in eating at pubs.

Jessica Vickers (7)
Wombridge Primary School, Oakengates

Just Be You!

A kennings poem

I am a...
Sports player,
Pizza lover,
Water treader,
Sleep doer,
Early riser,
Humongous dolphin lover,
Big chit-chatter,
Great bike rider,
Trampoline master,
And finally,
Excited learner.
And that is me.
Just be you!

Jackson Beddow (8)

Wombridge Primary School, Oakengates

This Is Me!

To make me my football-loving self you will need to follow this recipe:

A dab of touch of skill
A pinch of players
A gallon of cheers
A hint of white on the kit
A trace of goals
A pennyworth of boots

This makes *me, me!*

Riley Gill (11)

Wombridge Primary School, Oakengates

This Is Me

First you need love.
Add a loving friend with a hot cocoa and a scoop of marshmallows.
Add a gallon of kindness and mix in some fun memories.
Stir me up!
Place me into the oven and cook.
Don't forget to sprinkle icing sugar so I'm sweet.

Kai Williams (10)

Wombridge Primary School, Oakengates

This Is Me

This is me,
I'd say I'm quite passionate,
Sometimes I can be compassionate.

With me there is a spot of loyalty,
People say I have a lot of maturity,
When I do something kind I do it generously.

This is what makes me, me!

Joseph Reynolds (10)
Wombridge Primary School, Oakengates

Untitled

I am a lightning bolt,
I show kindness and respect,
I like partying,
I am tall like a giraffe,
I like playing with my friends,
I love cakes,
I like cheese like a mouse,
My hair is brown,
I love who I am,
It all makes me, me.

Leena Abu Hanifa Sadik (9)
Wombridge Primary School, Oakengates

A Recipe For Heavenly

First, gather kindness and honesty
Stir in tasty, warm sushi
Season with going on vacation
Add a pinch of happy disco music
Pour on going to the theatre
Mix in grateful and brave
Then warm gently with hot, spicy noodles.

Heavenly Ofori (7)
Wombridge Primary School, Oakengates

Hello, I Am Aaron

I am a whizz on the hockey pitch,
I really love sport,
I am a cheetah playing in games,
My speed is unmatched,
My favourite food is pizza,
I am nine years old,
My name is Aaron,
And this is me!

Aaron Joshi (9)
Wombridge Primary School, Oakengates

Just Be You

A kennings poem

I am...
A good helper,
An animal lover,
A pro gamer,
A long snoozer,
I am smart,
A Halloween lover,
A chit-chatter,
A YouTube watcher,
And finally,
I am me.
Just be you.

Noah Jones (8)
Wombridge Primary School, Oakengates

Party Charlie

My name is Charlie,
And I like to party,
My music is pop,
When it plays my body just can't stop,
I like to sing my lungs out,
And have a good scream and shout,
Pair this with fast food,
And I'm in the best mood.

Charlie Ricketts (9)
Wombridge Primary School, Oakengates

Just Be You

A kennings poem

I am a...
Great bike rider,
Game player,
Early riser,
Light sleeper,
Careful sports player,
Snake lover,
Home-made cake eater,
Fortnite player,
Lazy boy,
Friend helper.

Luciano Lomas (9)
Wombridge Primary School, Oakengates

I Am Me!

I am a...

Sporty person
Footballer
Football watcher
Painter
Basketballer
Mathematician
Writer
Sister
Swimmer
Late sleeper

I am me!

Lily-jean Ricketts (10)
Wombridge Primary School, Oakengates

I Am Me!

I am...

A book reader
An artist
A kind friend
Lovely
Smart
A loving child
Hopeful
Happy
Excited

I am *me!*

Rozalea Lomas (11)
Wombridge Primary School, Oakengates

I Am Me

I am...
Brother
Policeman
Chef
Funny person
Happy child
I am me!

Liam Studholme (9)
Wombridge Primary School, Oakengates

YOUNG WRITERS INFORMATION

We hope you have enjoyed reading this book – and that you will continue to in the coming years.

If you're the parent or family member of an enthusiastic poet or story writer, do visit our website **www.youngwriters.co.uk/subscribe** and sign up to receive news, competitions, writing challenges and tips, activities and much, much more! There's lots to keep budding writers motivated!

If you would like to order further copies of this book, or any of our other titles, then please give us a call or order via your online account.

Young Writers
Remus House
Coltsfoot Drive
Peterborough
PE2 9BF
(01733) 890066
info@youngwriters.co.uk

Join in the conversation!
Tips, news, giveaways and much more!

 **YoungWritersUK**    **YoungWritersCW**    **youngwriterscw**

Scan me to watch the
This Is Me video!